The **Essential** Buyer's Guide

Hinckley Triumph

TRIPLES & FOURS

750, 900, 955, 1000, 1050, 1200 – 1991-2009

Your marque expert:
Peter Henshaw

T0150287

VELOCE PUBLISHING

THE PUBLISHER OF FINE AUTOMOTIVE BOOKS

Veloce's Essential Buyer's Guide Series

Alfa GT (Booker)
Alfa Romeo Spider Giulia (Booker & Talbott)
BMW GS (Henshaw)
BSA Bantam (Henshaw)
BSA 500 & 650 Twins (Henshaw)
Citroën 2CV (Paxton)
Citroën ID & DS (Heilig)
Fiat 500 & 600 (Bobbitt)
Ford Capri (Paxton)
Hinckley Triumph triples & fours 750, 900, 955, 1000, 1050, 1200 – 1991-2009 (Henshaw)
Honda SOHC fours (Henshaw)
Jaguar E-type 3.8 & 4.2-litre (Crespin)
Jaguar E-type V12 5.3-litre (Crespin)
Jaguar XJ 1995-2003 (Crespin)
Jaguar/Daimler XJ6, XJ12 & Sovereign (Crespin)
Jaguar/Daimler XJ40 (Crespin)
Jaguar XJ-S (Crespin)
MGB & MGB GT (Williams)
Mercedes-Benz 280SL-560DSL Roadsters (Bass)
Mercedes-Benz 'Pagoda' 230SL, 250SL & 280SL Roadsters & Coupés (Bass)
Mini (Paxton)
Morris Minor & 1000 (Newell)
Norton Commando (Henshaw)
Porsche 928 (Hemmings)
Rolls-Royce Silver Shadow & Bentley T-Series (Bobbitt)
Subaru Impreza (Hobbs)
Triumph Bonneville (Henshaw)
Triumph Stag (Mort & Fox)
Triumph TR6 (Williams)
VW Beetle (Cservenka & Copping)
VW Bus (Cservenka & Copping)
VW Golf GTI (Cservenka & Copping)

www.veloce.co.uk

First published in May 2010 by Veloce Publishing Limited, Veloce House, Parkway Farm Business Park, Middle Farm Way, Poundbury, Dorchester, Dorset, DT1 3AR, England.
Fax 01305 250479/e-mail info@veloce.co.uk/web www.veloce.co.uk or www.velocebooks.com.
ISBN: 978-1-845842-87-1 UPC: 6-36847-04287-5

Readers with ideas for automotive books, or books on other transport or related hobby subjects, are invited to write to the editorial director of Veloce Publishing at the above address.
British Library Cataloguing in Publication Data – A catalogue record for this book is available from the British Library.
Typesetting, design and page make-up all by Veloce Publishing Ltd on Apple Mac. Printed in India by Imprint Digital.

Introduction
– the purpose of this book

This book is intended to be a straightforward, practical guide to the marque that relaunched the British motorcycle industry – Triumph. It won't list all the correct colour combinations for each year, or analyse how Triumph at Hinckley arose from the ashes of Triumph of Meriden, but hopefully it will help you avoid buying a dud.

Back in 1983, when the old Meriden factory finally closed, it seemed like the British bike industry had finally rolled over and died. Few people even noticed that the rights to the name had been bought by an unknown house builder by the name of John Bloor. Seven years later, everyone knew that Triumph was back with an all-new range of liquid-cooled threes and fours powering the Trident roadster, Daytona sports bike, and Trophy tourer.

They weren't radical bikes, but nor were the new Triumphs simply copies of the Kawasaki GPz series, as is sometimes implied. Instead, they were a conservative amalgam of then-current best practice; over-engineered, some said, but that was meant as a compliment. What surprised everyone was just how well-made and reliable they were. Sales began to gather speed, and new variants like the Thunderbird, Speed Triple and Tiger were added. By the late 1990s, when these first carburettor-fed bikes with their steel spine-frames were gradually being replaced by a new generation of fuel-injected, alloy-framed machines, Triumph was a fully fledged manufacturer with a good reputation.

This 240,000-mile Trident is proof that Triumphs can withstand high mileages.

Today, the Hinckley-built Triumphs make a good secondhand buy. Hinckley's determination to distance itself from the bad old days meant that its bikes have usually been solidly made and well finished. Not even the earliest bikes have gained classic status yet, so prices are low, and there's a wide choice of good fuel-injected bikes around. Most have a varation on the 900/955cc three-cylinder engine, which surely is a design classic: a strong and torquey unit whose

The Triumph badge is an evocative one, and part of the attraction of these bikes.

distinctive wail at high revs sounds like nothing else. No doubt about it, there's something special about a Triumph, and as this book tries to show, they can make a good secondhand buy with very few inherent flaws.

Note: This book covers two families of bikes. The 1991-on carburettored machines are referred to as 'spine-frames,' and the 1997-on injected bikes as 'fuel-injected.'

A used Triumph, such as this ST, can make a reliable, all year round motorcycle.

Thanks

This book would never have been completed without the help of many people. First of all, Trevor Smith at Sprint Manufacturing and mechanic John Lovick both shared their in-depth knowledge of Hinckley Triumphs with me. Staff at Triumph dealer Three Cross Motorcycles were very helpful, as was Sandy at Triumph-ant. Roy Vincent of Roy Vincent Motorcycles in Warminster kindly allowed me to photograph bikes, as did staff at V&J Superbikes at Yeovil and Bridgwater.

And thanks to all those private owners who did exactly the same: Tonka Richardson, Rupert Reeves and Jerry Fox.

Contents

Essential Buyer's Guide™ currency

At the time of publication a BG unit of currency '⬤' equals aproximately £1.00/US$2.00/Euro 1.50. Please adjust to suit current exchange rates.

Tall and short riders

All Triumphs covered in this book are big, roomy bikes that suit six-footers. The downside is that the spine-frame bikes are tall and top heavy, so are intimidating for shorter riders and novices, the exceptions being the lower-seated Thunderbird and Legend. Fuel-injected bikes are more manageable.

955cc fuel-injected bikes can return 60-65mpg.

Running costs

Can be heavy on tyres, chains and brakes if you're a hard rider, and new spares are expensive. On the other hand, there's a good choice of secondhand spares, and consumables aren't particularly expensive. 955 fuel-injected bikes are the most economical, with 60-65mpg possible. The 1050s return around 50mpg, and the spine-frame bikes are thirstiest of all: 40-45mpg for a steady rider, 30-35mpg for the keen types.

Maintenance

Not onerous, with longish 6000-mile service intervals, with tappet checks and (advisably) cam chain replacement at higher mileages. Tyres and chains need to be checked regularly, as these are heavy bikes with lots of power. On the Thunderbird and Adventurer, there's a lot of chrome to keep pristine, and all bikes benefit from frequent washing to keep road salt at bay.

Usability

So long as you're comfortable with the weight and seat height, Triumphs are very usable day-to-day bikes, with the exception of the more committed 1997-on Daytonas. As a breed, they are roomy, comfortable, and often come with hard luggage.

Parts availability
Very good. The Hinckley factory still offers spares backup for all bikes, and there's a good selection of secondhand spares from breakers. Tyres and chains are in common sizes, and many of the electric and suspension parts are from major industry suppliers (Kayaba, Nippon Denso, etc).

Parts costs
Service parts are reasonable, but other parts are expensive, and can cost even more than equivalent spares for a Honda or Yamaha, for example. As mentioned above, working secondhand parts with some sort of warranty are a good, cheaper, alternative.

Insurance group
Big fast bikes, expensive to repair after a prang, aren't cheap to insure. The lowest insurance rating in the UK is the Thunderbird at group 11, then the spine-frame Tridents in group 12. Tiger is 13, Sprint ST 14, and Daytonas are in 14/15. The oldest bikes may be elegible for cheaper classic limited-mileage policies.

Investment potential
Limited, simply because Triumphs have sold well, and 18 years after the original launch there are lots of them around. Limited editions like the Daytona Super III, Speed Triple 750 and Daytona 1200 SE should go up in value, and the spine-frame Daytona 750 and 1000 will become collectable too.

Foibles
Very few. The Hinckley Triumphs were, and are, carefully designed, conventionally engineered bikes that aim to have mass appeal. The only long-running foible is the starter sprag clutch.

Plus points
Top of the list has to be the 885 or 955cc triple, a modern classic among motorcycle engines. There's also the appeal of the Triumph name, the bikes' fundamental reliability and well-sorted nature. Spine-frames and early injected bikes are good value.

Minus points
One man's broad appeal is another's lack of character (though that's hardly true of the Hinckley triple). Spine-frame bikes are tall and top heavy, new spares are expensive, and no Hinckley Triumph will be cheap to run.

Alternatives
Lots of these. We're covering a wide range of bikes here, so any of the Japanese/European equivalents should be considered. Particular counterparts that spring to mind are the Honda FireBlade (Daytona T595 and 955i), BMW GS (Tiger), Honda VFR800 (Sprint ST) and Suzuki Bandit 1200 (Trident 900).

2 Cost considerations
– affordable, or a money pit?

As mentioned earlier, older Triumphs may often be cheap to buy, but they won't be cheap to run. The spine-frame bikes are quite thirsty (though no worse than equivalent big bikes) and all will be relatively heavy on tyres, brakes and chains. For larger non-service items, buying secondhand is a good option (though there may not be a warranty). Service items are a reasonable price, but other spares are not cheap, though that's something shared with all the major marques. The major 12,000-mile service is a significant expense, but Triumph dealers will allow two days for the job, which includes changing the brake fluid as well as oil, filters and plugs and checking the tappets.

Spares prices
1994 Daytona 900 (serviceable secondhand parts)
Fairing panel – ⬤ x 35
Carburettor set – ⬤ x 160
Instrument set – ⬤ x 45
Forks (new stanchions/seals) – ⬤ x 295
Front wheel – ⬤ x 115
Brake disc – ⬤ x 70
Exhaust silencer – ⬤ x 115
Rear shock – ⬤ x 115 (recon – 230)
CDI unit - ⬤ x 170

2009 Sprint ST 1050 (new parts)
Oil filter – ⬤ x 9
Air filter – ⬤ x 23
Brake pads – ⬤ x 18 both sides
Front tyre (Bridgestone) – ⬤ x 76
Rear tyre (Bridgestone) – ⬤ x 96
Chain/sprocket set – ⬤ x 140
Clutch lever – ⬤ x 24

Fairing side panel – ⬤ x 287
Clutch (complete) – ⬤ x 523
Starter motor – ⬤ x 407
Silencer – ⬤ x 312
Rear shock – ⬤ x 534
ECU – ⬤ x 1090

Servicing
6000 miles
  – ⬤ x 160
12,000 miles
  – ⬤ x 480

Tyre wear can be a major expense.

Breakers are a good source of non-service items.

Service parts like brake pads aren't expensive.

3 Living with a Hinckley Triumph
– will you get along together?

Hinckley Triumphs are quite easy bikes to live with: not demanding to ride, not finicky in their service demands, and reasonably practical as day-to-day transport. A spine-frame bike won't cost much to buy and will happily run all year round, as many of them do, and both they and the fuel-injected Triumphs can rack up high mileages without big repair bills.

Don't be put off by high mileage.

The big plus is that this is a complete range of bikes – roadster, tourer, cruiser, sports bike and street fighter – all based around the same characterful three-cylinder engine. Hinckley's other engines – the 750cc triple and the 1000/1200cc fours – get very little attention for the very good reason that the 885/955cc three is a real gem. It's very torquey and relaxed, yet feels as much at home powering a sports bike as a roadster. Unlike the more frenetic Japanese fours, it has a slightly rough-edged feel that is very appealing, though thanks to the balancer shafts, it's also quite smooth. With the exception of the cruisers (all in 69bhp form) it's also powerful enough to be entertaining, and to cover big distances at high speed, if that's what you want. If you like that triple (and most riders do once they've tried one) there should be a bike in the range that suits.

Later Daytonas and naked Speed Triples apart, Triumphs are comfortable over distance. These are physically big bikes, with plenty of room for two people and lots of luggage, a genuinely different alternative to, say, a Harley V-twin or a Honda Pan-European. There is a downside to the size issue though. The spine-frame Triumphs in particular are heavy machines – in fact, they feel top-heavy because of the substantial steel backbone frame and large mass of the motor. Combined with a high, wide-ish seat (something that applies to all Tigers), the result can be intimidating and awkward at low speeds, especially for those with short legs. Out of town this is hardly a problem, but it needs bearing in mind, and it puts more emphasis on the test ride. The exceptions are the cruisers, which start out with lower seats (only 725mm on the Legend) which make a great deal of difference.

Spine-frame Triumphs are tall, heavy machines.

The fuel-injected bikes are far better in this respect. A Sprint ST weighs 13kg less than a Trophy 900, and also carries its weight lower down. It's still a substantial machine, but is far easier to manage, and the Speed Triple in particular is an easy bike to hop on and ride with confidence straight away. All the Triumphs handle well, though few would argue that the original spine-frame Daytonas could rival a FireBlade – they're far too heavy for that. Given respect for their mass, the spine-frame bikes are secure handlers, and the fuel-injected generation is very good indeed.

Maintenance isn't too onerous, thanks to 6000-mile service intervals and thoroughly conventional engineering that doesn't need any special treatment. Routine servicing, such as oil/filter changes, brake pads and chains, are all fairly straightforward, well within the scope of a competent home mechanic.

If anything does detract from this picture, it's that all the Triumphs are heavy, powerful bikes, which inevitably takes its toll on consumables. Much of this depends on riding style, but owners

All big bikes are heavy on consumables.

need to keep on top of tyre wear and chain/sprocket condition. Looking after chain drive is a chore compared to shaft-drive alternatives such as the BMW, especially on the touring Trophy. An automatic chain oiler is a sign of a fastidious, probably high-mileage, previous owner. For top fuel economy, the 955cc fuel-injected bikes are best, with 60-65mpg possible, and Sprint ST 955 owners can expect a tank range of 200+ miles. The later 1050s use more fuel, and the spine-frames more still. But let's not overstate any of this – all big bikes are heavy on consumables, and the Triumphs are no better or worse than most of them.

Hinckley Triumphs have been around long enough now for a huge fund of knowledge to have built up, and there are plenty of owners clubs and forums out there with fellow owners willing to help out. The long-running Triumph Owners Motorcycle Club (www.tomcc.org) is open to owners of Hinckley bikes, and links up with associated clubs all around the world. The official factory club is RAT (Riders Association of Triumph), which has a very active forum as well as lots of events. There are other web forums (see the back of this book for details) and the Tiger is especially well served here.

There's something else about Hinckley Triumphs that makes them good to live with. They are particularly tough and long-lived bikes, able to run high mileages with only routine maintenance. Fifty thousand miles is no problem at all, and there are several running around with six figures showing – some couriers have clocked up 250,000 miles with no major problems. Like any bike, they need looking after, and respond to a caring owner, but the Triumph tank badge effectively brings dependable technology in a distinctive range of bikes with an engine that's like nothing else available at the price – perhaps the best argument for having one in the garage.

4 Relative values
– which model for you?

This chapter also looks at the strengths and weaknesses of each model, so that you can decide which is best for you. Hinckley Triumph evolution divides into two, the two families of bikes sharing very little in terms of actual parts. Spine-frame bikes were built from 1991 to 2004, and all use the carburettor-fed versions of Triumph's three- and four-cylinder engines, mounted in a substantial steel backbone frame. From 1997, these were supplanted by the new generation of fuel-injected bikes, three-cylinders only, with aluminium alloy frames, and the latest 1050s are a development of these.

Models

Spine-frames
Trident 750 1991-98
Trident 900 1991-98
Sprint 900 1993-98
Trophy 900 1991-2001
Trophy 1200 1991-2003
Speed Triple 750 1996
Speed Triple 900 1994-96
Daytona 750 1991-93
Daytona 900 1993-96
Daytona Super III 1994-96
Daytona 1000 1991-93
Daytona 1200 1993-98
Thunderbird 900 1995-2003
Thunderbird Sport 900 1995-2005

Adventurer 900 1996-2001
Legend TT 900 1998-2001
Tiger 900 1993-98

Fuel-injected
Daytona T595 1997-98
Speed Triple T509 1997-98
Daytona 955i 1999-2007
Speed Triple 955i 1999-2004
Sprint ST 955i 1999-04
Sprint RS 955i 2000-03
Sprint ST 1050 2005-to date
Speed Triple 1050 2004-to date
Tiger 955i 2001-07
Tiger 1050 2007-to date

Spine-frames

The first thing to say about the spine-frame Triumphs is that, under the skin, they are all very similar indeed. When Hinckley Triumph started production in 1991, it couldn't afford to launch a complete range of different bikes all in one go. So it adopted the modular approach, with a full range sharing many common parts to cut costs. Six bikes were unveiled at the Cologne Show, with four engines: 750 and 900 triples, 1000 and 1200 fours. All shared the same 55mm bore, the same basic layout, and the same steel backbone frame. Even the wiring loom was identical on the very early bikes, and the only concession to the different geometry required by a sports bike and a tourer was catered for by different steering yoke offset.

This comprehensive parts sharing enabled Triumph to launch a complete range of bikes, while minimising development, production, and parts costs. It also means, incidentally, that any early engine will fit any early backbone frame, so if you're bored with your lowly Trident 750, it should be possible to convert it to a 900 or even 1200 without any cutting and shutting.

The disadvantage is that the bikes were slightly compromised – the Daytonas were really too heavy and cumbersome to make true sports bikes, while the Trophys lacked the shaft drive of a serious tourer. As time went on, Triumph did begin to differentiate more – higher bars and lower footrests for the Trident and Trophy, for example.

A basic Trident is the cheapest route to Hinckley Triumph ownership.

Bright yellow spine-frame Daytona has presence!

Trident

The basic, naked spine-frame Hinckley Triumph, offered in 750 and 900cc three-cylinder form only. The 900 soon became the road testers' favourite, and the customers' too, outselling the 750 by about five to one – 750s come up for sale very rarely. After two years, they were revamped with those higher bars and lower footrests, plus more traditional colour schemes with pinstriping, and a black finish engine.

They were joined by the Trident Sprint, basically the 900 with a twin headlamp half-fairing, which became a well thought of model in its own right, a good all rounder with some of the weather protection of a Trophy but slightly less weight. It received better suspension for 1996, and was joined two years later by the Sprint Sports and Sprint Executive, which only lasted a year.

Trident 750 – 49%
Trident 900 – 56%
Sprint 900 – 49%

1996-on twin-headlight Trophy.

Trophy

The Trophy was ostensibly the tourer of the range, with 900 triple or 1200 four power and a full fairing with a clock, though at first it had no standard luggage, a low screen and lowish bars. The big 110bhp 1200 got good reviews at launch time, but as with the Trident, it was the 900 triple that found more fans.

Gradually, the Trophy did become more of a proper tourer, being given a major revamp in early 1996, which brought a much larger, more protective twin-headlamp fairing and taller screen, plus colour-matched panniers. At the same time the 1200 was given taller gearing in an effort to improve fuel consumption. The 900 Trophy hung on until 2002, the 1200 remaining on sale for another

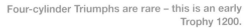

Four-cylinder Triumphs are rare – this is an early Trophy 1200.

year. They remained heavyweight machines to the end, though the chain-drive really hampered their role as serious tourers.

Trophy 900 – 77%
Trophy 1200 – 96%

The Speed Triple gives the raw three-cylinder experience.

Speed Triple

Trident, Trophy, and the Daytona were all aimed at well established market sectors, but the Speed Triple arguably pioneered a new one – the factory café racer/street fighter. It was a simple formula, basically the Daytona 900, with its low bars and rearset footrests, but with no fairing and a single round headlamp. It also had a five-speed gearbox, rather than the Daytona's standard six-speed.

Launched for 1994, the bike was an instant hit, and as the basic Trident began to fade into the background, it was the Speed Triple that delivered the Triumph three-cylinder experience in its most raw, wind-blown form. And the name was a simple but clever reference to the old Triumph's seminal Speed Twin of 1937. Offered in black, yellow or orange, the Speed Triple made a bold statement, though there were few changes apart from the addition of a six-speed gearbox and revised suspension for 1996, its final year.

At the same time, a rare 750cc derivative was launched. With the new fuel-injected range on the horizon, Triumph decided it needed to use up stocks of the 750 triple more quickly, and a 750 Speed Triple was a good limited-edition ploy, lasting for just one year. It didn't have the torque-laden dynamics of the 900, but the baby Speed Triple is worth looking out for, if only for its rarity value.

Speed Triple 900 – 60%

Daytona

Of all the new Hinckley Triumphs, the Daytonas were the only ones to receive a lukewarm reception. Not only were they too tall and heavy to be true sports bikes, but the engine choice was 750 triple or 1000 four, both of them short-stroke versions that lacked the sheer drive of the long-stroke 900 and 1200. One journalist tellingly wrote that while the 900cc triple could be mistaken for a full-litre power unit, the 1000 four felt more like a 750, with little power below 8000rpm. So these very first Daytonas didn't sell well, and lasted only two years, though as with the 750 Speed Triple, that makes them interesting finds secondhand.

The Daytona was effectively relaunched for 1993, with the now revered 900 triple motor and a restyle (upswept pipe and lower screen) that gave it a sportier look, helped by dropping the old Daytona's graphic-heavy bodywork in favour of plain yellow, red or blue (later black).

The Daytona Super III could be a future collector's item.

It was joined a year later by the Super III, with which Triumph made a determined attempted to make a real sports bike out of the spine-frame chassis. Cosworth Engineering helped tune the 900 triple up to 113bhp, Triumph's own six-piston calipers radically improved the brakes, and the addition of some carbon fibre parts shaved a couple of kilos off the weight. Offered in yellow/black or all-black, and up to October 1995, the Super III is a rare bike that should become one of the more collectable Daytonas in the future, though it was still no match for a FireBlade.

Early Daytonas are more sports-tourers than out-and-out sports bikes.

The ultimate spine-frame Daytona (at least in terms of outright power and speed) was the 1200, launched for 1993 as a 147bhp heavyweight projectile, at a time when Japanese importers were voluntarily restricting their bikes to 125bhp. This biggest Daytona of all had revised suspension for 1996, and it's worth looking out for the special edition SE of 1999, for the final run of 250 bikes. These feature six-pot calipers, black/gold paintwork, pillion seat cover, and a numbered plaque.

Daytona 750/1000 – 50%
Daytona 900 – 51%
Daytona 1200 – 55%
Daytona Super III – 58%

Thunderbird/Adventurer/Legend

With Triumph's strong heritage, it was only a matter of time before Hinckley chose to cash in on it. With a new rear subframe and retro styling, the Thunderbird put the 900 triple into a 1950s set of clothes, right down to the mouth organ tank badge. With lots of chrome, it certainly looked the part, and the familiar triple was detuned to 69bhp for its new cruiser role, while the gearbox lost its sixth speed.

Launched in January 1995, the T'bird was joined by the Adventurer later that year, the same basic bike but with Harley-influenced styling. This acquired a 19in front wheel for 1999, and an orange/black colour scheme in January 2001. The Legend TT, launched in May 1998, was intended as an entry level cruiser, with less chrome, a single-colour paintwork and lower 725mm seat. It was soon (for '99) upgraded with red/silver or green/silver paint as the Legend De Luxe, and for 2001 reverted to a single colour of red, green or black. By then it was nearly £1000 cheaper than the Thunderbird, though the secondhand difference in value is small.

The most significant addition to the

The Legend TT and Thunderbird make for a different sort of cruiser.

T'bird range was the Thunderbird Sport, which married retro styling with a more sporting chassis. The triple was boosted to 82bhp, gained a sixth gear, lower bars, and Speed Triple forks and twin front discs. In yellow/black or red/black, the Sport was offered right up to 2005, the last surviving spine-frame bike, and acquired something of a cult following.

Thunderbird – 103%
Adventurer – 88%
Legend TT – 92%
Thunderbird Sport – 117%

Flamboyant graphics mark the early Tiger.

The Tiger isn't a true off-road machine, but makes a great road bike.

Tiger

Triumph's stab at the BMW GS market was unveiled in October 1998. Less of a true off-roader than the GS, it aped the style of a big enduro very well. The 900 triple was detuned to 82bhp and mounted in a chassis with longer wheelbase, higher seat (if short in the leg, don't bother), and new nylon fuel tank, with the 'Tiger' script scrawled across the twin-headlight fairing and side panels

It might be too big and heavy to be a serious off-road bike (though a competent rider could take the Tiger onto the dirt), but the Tiger proved to be a great road bike, torquey and comfortable. It was a sales hit in Germany; quite a compliment in the land of the GS. Colours were blue, yellow, black, or later, British Racing Green.
Tiger 900 – 83%

Fuel-injected
Daytona/Speed Triple

Nineteen ninety-seven was a milestone year for Triumph. The new fuel-injected T595 Daytona and T509 Speed Triple were virtually all-new, now with aluminium-alloy frame, fuel-injected, three-cylinder engine (on the same format as before, but effectively a new engine), and swoopy new styling. Unlike previous Daytonas, this new one could compete on equal terms with the Honda FireBlade and Ducati 916, and it sold well. Meanwhile, the Speed Triple (with a sleeved-down 885cc version of the Daytona's 955cc triple) created its famous bug-eyed style that looked like nothing else.

A bug-eyed Speed Triple 955i.

Both these bikes offer a quite different riding experience to the earlier spine-frames, lighter, with more nimble handling and impressive performance, while the new three-cylinder engine sounds just as distinctive as the old one. Both were updated as 955i's for 1999 (the Speed Triple gaining the 955cc motor), and the Daytona gained a stainless exhaust in March 2000, more power (147bhp) in 2001 and a single-sided swing arm for '03. Triumph's sports bike lasted until 2007, but was increasingly left behind in this fast-moving market.

The Speed Triple, on the other hand, was secure in its own niche, and continued to offer the intoxicating mix of that three-cylinder motor in a naked bike with outlandish styling. Power was boosted to 118bhp for 2002, and there was a special edition all-black bike in '04. The following year, it gained the new 1050cc triple, which in turn was boosted to 131bhp in 2007.

Daytona T595 – 68%
Daytona 955i – 109%
Speed Triple T509 – 86%
Speed Triple 955i – 127%

Lower bars on the Sprint RS.

The RS is a cheaper, sportier version of the Sprint ST.

The Sprint ST1050 is faster, but uses more fuel than the 955.

Sprint ST/RS

The Sprint ST was a softer, sports-touring version of the Daytona, with a simpler twin-beam frame and the triple detuned to 108bhp. It became the classic sports-tourer, more than a match for Honda's benchmark VFR: fast, comfy and with a good fuel range, it was everything a good sports tourer should be. It shared the Daytona's single-sided swing arm.

The Sprint RS was launched in 2000 as a cheaper version, with half (not full) fairing and a cheaper double-sided swing arm (which also saved about 9kg). It lacked the ST's swivelling

955i ST makes a characterful alternative to a Honda VFR.

exhaust (to make space for panniers) but was a slightly sportier bike. Both RS and ST were boosted to 118bhp for 2002, and two years later the ST was fitted with panniers, heated grips and a rear rack as standard.

Big news for 2005 was the 1050cc triple, which saw the ST launched with new styling and the choice of silver or blue paintwork. Power went up to 125bhp in 2007 (when red joined the colour choices) and ABS was an option.

Sprint RS – 83%
Sprint ST 955i – 112%
Sprint ST 1050 – 200%

Tiger 955i/1050

The Tiger got the fuel-injection treatment for 2001, with new styling, black and green colours and more road-oriented nature. At first it came with spoked wheels, like the original Tiger, but gained cast wheels for 2004, along with standard panniers, heated grips and a centre stand. The Tiger was effectively a comfortable tourer, though given a determined and competent rider, it really could be taken off road.

For 2007 the Tiger was restyled for the 1050cc triple, and by 2008 it was offered in base, ABS or SE versions. The latter came with ABS brakes, colour-matched panniers and handguards and Matt Graphite or Matt Black colours.

Tiger 955i – 149%
Tiger 1050 – 215%

The Tiger 955i made another good tourer, but could also tackle green lanes.

The Tiger 1050 is more road-biased than ever.

5 Before you view
– be well informed

To avoid a wasted journey, and the disappointment of finding that the bike does not match your expectations, it will help if you're very clear about what questions you want to ask before you pick up the phone. Some of these points might appear basic, but when you're excited about the prospect of buying your dream classic, it's amazing how some of the most obvious things slip the mind. Also check the current values of the model in which you are interested in the classic bike magazine classified ads.

Where is the bike?
Is it going to be worth travelling to the next county/state, or even across a border? A locally advertised machine, although it may not sound very interesting, can add to your knowledge for very little effort, so make a visit – it might even be in better condition than expected.

Dealer or private sale?
Establish early on if the bike is being sold by its owner or by a trader. A private owner should have all the history, so don't be afraid to ask detailed questions. A dealer may have more limited knowledge of the bike's history, but should have some documentation. A dealer may offer a warranty/guarantee (ask for a printed copy).

Cost of collection and delivery?
A dealer may well be used to quoting for delivery. A private owner may agree to meet you halfway, but only agree to this after you have seen the bike at the vendor's address to validate the documents. Conversely, you could meet halfway and agree the sale, but insist on meeting at the vendor's address for the handover.

View – when and where?
It is always preferable to view at the vendor's home or business premises. In the case of a private sale, the bike's documentation should tally with the vendor's name and address. Arrange to view only in daylight, and avoid a wet day – the vendor may be reluctant to let you take a test ride if it's wet.

Reason for sale?
Do make it one of the first questions. Why is the bike being sold and how long has it been with the current owner? How many previous owners?

Condition?
Ask for an honest appraisal of the bike's condition. Ask specifically about some of the check items described in Chapter 8.

All original specification?
An all-original specification isn't such an issue for a Hinckley Triumph as it is for an older classic bike. 'Sensible' extras such as hard luggage, screen and heated grips will increase the value (especially if they're Triumph items). On the Daytonas and Speed Triples, add-on carbon fibre and aftermarket exhausts will not.

Matching data/legal ownership?

Do frame, engine numbers and licence plate match the official registration document? Is the owner's name and address recorded in the official registration documents?

For those countries that require an annual test of roadworthiness, does the bike have a document showing it complies (an MoT certificate in the UK, which can be verified on 0845 600 5977)?

Does the bike carry a current road fund licence/licence plate tag? If not, in the UK it should have a SORN (Statutory Off Road Notification) certificate.

Does the vendor own the bike outright? Money might be owed to a finance company or bank: the bike could even be stolen. Several organisations will supply the data on ownership, based on the bike's licence plate number, for a fee. Such companies can often also tell you whether the bike has been 'written off' by an insurance company. In the UK these organisations can supply vehicle data:
HPI – 01722 422 422 – www.hpicheck.com
AA – 0870 600 0836 – www.theaa.com
RAC – 0870 533 3660 – www.rac.co.uk
Other countries will have similar organisations.

Insurance

Check with your existing insurer before setting out – your current policy might not cover you if you do buy the bike and decide to ride it home.

How can you pay?

A cheque/check will take several days to clear and the seller may prefer to sell to a cash buyer. However, a banker's draft (a cheque issued by a bank) is as good as cash, but safer, so contact your own bank and become familiar with the formalities that are necessary to obtain one.

Buying at auction?

If the intention is to buy at auction see Chapter 10 for further advice.

Professional vehicle check (mechanical examination)

There are often marque/model specialists who will undertake professional examination of a vehicle on your behalf. Owners clubs may be able to put you in touch with such specialists.

6 Inspection equipment
– these items will really help

This book
Before you rush out of the door, gather together a few items that will help as you work your way around the bike. This book is designed to be your guide at every step, so take it along and use the check boxes in Chapter 9 to help you assess each area of the bike you're interested in. Don't be afraid to let the seller see you using it.

Reading glasses (if you need them for close work)
Take your reading glasses if you need them to read documents and make close-up inspections.

Overalls
Be prepared to get dirty. Take along a pair of overalls, if you have them.

Camera
Take a digital camera so that later you can study some areas of the bike more closely. Take a picture of any part of the bike that causes you concern, and seek a friend's opinion.

A friend, preferably a knowledgeable enthusiast
Ideally, have a friend come along too, and if they know their Triumphs, so much the better; a second opinion is always valuable.

– walk away or stay?

General condition

First impressions count. Does the bike look well cared for, or neglected? A bit of honest dirt is no problem on an older high-mileage machine, but damaged nuts and allen bolts are signs of a less than sympathetic owner. Check for signs of crash damage – are the engine cases, forks, silencer or handlebar ends scraped on one side of the bike? If they are, ask the seller how this happened. At the steering head, check to see if the steering stops on the lower clamp are bent or dented, a sure sign of an accident.

Some bikes are obviously battle-scarred ...

Try pushing the bike forwards a few metres, and back again. It should roll freely on a flat surface – if it doesn't, it's likely that the brake calipers are sticking and will need a strip down and clean, or even replacing.

What extras are fitted? An automatic chain oiler suggests a contientious owner, while a taller screen and hard luggage indicate a higher mileage tourer. If the bike has an aftermarket silencer, is it road legal?

It's worth remembering that a cosmetically challenged bike may well be perfectly sound underneath, something that should be clear during the test ride. But a tatty appearance should be reflected in the price.

Engine/frame numbers

Do the VINs (Vehicle Identification Numbers) tally with those on the documentation? (See page 24 for VIN locations). If they don't, you may just be looking at a bike that has had an engine swap that was never recorded in the paperwork, or it could have been built up from stolen parts. If the owner doesn't have a convincing explanation, go home – there are plenty of Triumphs on the market.

Check that the VINs tally with the documentation.

Documentation

If the seller claims to be the bike's owner, make sure he/she really is by checking the registration document, which, in the UK, is the V5C. The person listed on the V5C isn't necessarily the legal owner, but their details should match those of whoever is selling the bike. Also use the V5C to check the engine/frame VINs.

An annual roadworthiness certificate – the MoT in the UK – is handy proof that the bike was roadworthy when tested, and a whole sheaf of them are evidence of the bike's history – when it was actively being used, and what the mileage was at test time. The more of these come with the bike, the better.

Engine

Start the engine, from cold if possible. Does the starter engage cleanly? If it just spins over without engaging at all, or tries to hit home with a clunk, then the starter sprag clutch is worn out. This isn't an expensive item, but getting to it is a big job, especially on 1994-2001 bikes, where it entails taking the engine out of the frame, which could cost ●x500, plus parts at a Triumph dealer. It's an easier job on pre-1994 and post-2001 bikes, and it's far less common on later machines in any case.

First impressions count, but take a good close look.

Listen to the engine running. Expect plenty of rustle and whirr on early spine-frames, but rattling could be an out of adjustment balance shaft (four-cylinder engine) or snapped alternator shaft bolts (all engines, pre-2002). Blip the throttle – there should be no blue smoke, a sign of general top end wear.

Suspension/tyres

Check the front forks for oil leaks, pitting or rusting. With the bike on its centre stand (if fitted), check for play in the forks by grasping the bottom of the legs and trying to rock them back and forth. Take the bike off the stand, hold the front brake on and pump the forks up and down – they should move smoothly and without squeaks or rattles. Sit on the bike to check the rear suspension – as with the forks, the shock should move smoothly and quietly. If it feels oversoft (bearing in mind the pre-load setting) then it could need replacing.

Tyres are easy to check, and well worn rubber is a good means of levering down the price. Bikes used for a lot of motorway miles will have worn a flat in the centre of the tyre – this upsets the handling and means you'll have to replace the tyre soon.

Tyre condition is easy to assess.

Does the starter motor work first time? If it just spins (without turning the engine over) or clunks, then there is probably sprag clutch trouble. Best tested when the engine is cold, as it often doesn't show up when it's warm.

Look for signs of crash damage. It's likely that an older, high mileage bike will have been down at some point in its life, if only at low speed. If there is evidence, think about this on the test ride – is the bike running straight and true, including under braking?

Watch for misfiring, which could signal imminent coil failure. And if the engine dies after about 10 minutes from cold, the ignition pick-up is the most likely cause – a simple and cheap component, but the fairing has to come off for access.

Brake calipers will stick if used through the winter and not cleaned. The underslung rear caliper on some Daytonas suffers the most, so if the brakes appear to be binding, a sticky caliper is the most likely cause.

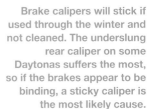

Engine paint can flake off, allowing the alloy to corrode. It looks unslightly, though underneath there may be a mechanically fine motorcycle. Still, it will be more difficult to sell when the time comes, so expect the price to reflect the appearance.

9 Serious evaluation
– 30 minutes for years of enjoyment

Score each section as follows: 4 = excellent; 3 = good; 2 = average; 1 = poor
The totting up procedure is detailed at the end of the chapter. Be realistic in your marking!

Engine/frame numbers

The first job is to check whether the VIN (Vehicle Identification Number) for engine and frame tally with those on the documentation. If they don't, make your excuses

The engine VIN is easy to find.

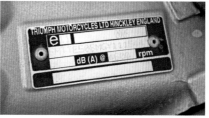

VIN plate.

Engine VIN on right-hand side of crankcase.

and walk away. On spine-frames the VIN frame number is found on the right-hand side of the steering head, and on UK bikes also on a VIN plate riveted to the frame under the seat. The engine VIN is on the upper crankcase, right-hand side. On fuel-injected bikes, the engine VIN is in the same place, and the frame VIN is on the right-hand side of the steering head, though on Daytonas, Speed Triples and Sprints, the VIN plate is riveted there as well. On the Tiger, the VIN plate is found on

Frame VIN on steering head.

the frame under the seat, just to the rear of the battery. If the numbers don't match, there could be a legitimate reason, though the documentation should have been amended to suit.

Paint/alloy/chrome

If there's one thing just about everyone is agreed on, it's that Triumph's finish is pretty good, partly a result of Hinckley's determination to disassociate itself from Meriden's poor reputation. But don't let this lull you into a false sense of security – if neglected, a Hinckley Triumph will start to look tatty, just like any other bike.

Chrome on cruisers can deteriorate.

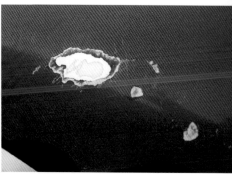

Triumph paintwork is good, and this sort of wear is rare.

If a bike has been cared for it will be obvious ...

... but alloy can corrode.

Nevertheless, the paintwork is good, with thick, tough plastic bodywork (actually thought to be better on the early bikes than the latest Sprint ST 1050). On older bikes, expect it be faded and with the odd scratch – but that's hardly a serious problem. Peeling paint on the engine and frame looks bad, but it's purely cosmetic, though it should still be reflected in the price and is some indication of the care given by previous owners.

Plain alloy parts will corrode if not washed regularly, and if looking at a Thunderbird, Legend or Adventurer, take a good look at the abundant chrome used on these bikes (though the Legend had less of it). The indicator stalks on early T'birds are prone to bubbling corrosion – Triumph later changed suppliers, and then it's less of an issue. Don't forget to check chrome wheel rims. Again, a well looked after bike (some of the cruisers will hardly have been out in the rain, but don't count on it) should be fine.

Bodywork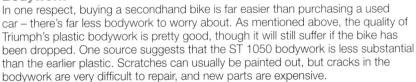

In one respect, buying a secondhand bike is far easier than purchasing a used car – there's far less bodywork to worry about. As mentioned above, the quality of Triumph's plastic bodywork is pretty good, though it will still suffer if the bike has been dropped. One source suggests that the ST 1050 bodywork is less substantial than the earlier plastic. Scratches can usually be painted out, but cracks in the bodywork are very difficult to repair, and new parts are expensive.

Bodywork is well finished and substantial.

Plastic, especially on spine-frames, is thick.

The good news is that bike breakers are a source of secondhand bodywork, and there is a reasonable supply for most models. Cracked plastic is no reason to reject a bike, as long as the damage is reflected in the price, and you are prepared to search for a replacement panel and fit it – it may also need repainting to match the rest of the bike. Damaged bodywork could also indicate more serious damage elsewhere on the bike, so treat it as a clue to look for more bad news, such as bent or snapped footpegs and levers, scraped engine cases and exhaust silencer.

Crashbars are a worthwhile option on the naked bikes – the Trident, Speed Triple and the cruisers – and again, examine these for scrapes and knocks. Tigers also have a bashplate to protect the underside of the engine – very few of the bikes will have been ridden off-road, but it's worth checking the bashplate for damage just the same.

Badges/graphics

Badges are an important aspect of any Triumph, simply because there's a lot of ownership pride in the name. The non-cruisers use stick-on badges that last very well and don't appear to suffer from peeling or fading. Some of the older model-specific badging may be more difficult to get hold of now, such as the early Tiger's loud and lairy 'signature' across the bodywork.

Cruisers, going for the traditional Triumph look, use screwed-on metal tank badges, which look wonderful but can be unscrewed as well ... Fortunately,

Original badges and graphics last well.

They may be tricky to replace, though.

replacements are available, though make sure you get the right one for the particular model. The Thunderbird used Triumph's 1950s-style 'mouth organ' tank badge, the Adventurer the 1960s-style badge, and the Legend: a much simpler badge featuring just the Triumph name.

Seat

All Triumphs had a dual seat, though the rare Daytona Super III added a pillion seat cover to give the bike a solo seat look, and this was optional on all Speed Triples. If this cover is there, check it's firmly in place and that the finish matches the rest of the bodywork. The actual style of the seat varies hugely, and cruisers may also have an optional pillion backrest and/or king and queen style seat.

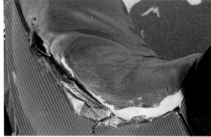

Seats can be recovered and restored.

Most seats are still intact.

As on any bike, the main seat cover will split eventually, which of course allows rain in, which the foam padding soaks up – and once seat foam gets wet, it never dries out, giving you a permamently damp backside, or a rock hard seat on icy mornings. New covers and complete seats in various styles are available, though recovering an old seat is a specialist job.

Only the Legend has a truly low seat, but if you find the other bikes a little tall for short legs, then a seat specialist will be able to cut the seat down for you, and recover it.

Rubbers

A good guide to the mileage of a secondhand car is wear on the pedal rubbers, and the same goes for a bike, though in this case look at the footrest and gearlever

Worn rubber cover is a good indication of hours on the road.

Check footrests for wear.

rubbers, and the handlebar grips. All Triumphs had rubber pads on the footrests (even the Tiger) so well worn or torn examples indicate high mileage, which may or may not concur with what the mileometer or the owner is claiming! Of course, rubbers can be replaced, so this isn't an infallible method – look for suspiciously new rubbers on an otherwise well used bike.

Frame

4 3 2 1

Spine-frame is of thick steel, and very strong.

The most important job here is to check whether the main frame is straight and true. Crash damage may have bent it, putting the wheels out of line. One way of checking is by using an experienced eye and taut string, but the surest way to ascertain a frame's straightness is on the test ride – any serious misalignment should be obvious in the way the bike handles.

Check the steering head for damage and flaking paint.

The fuel-injected Sprint ST/RS frame is completely different to that of the Daytona/Speed Triple.

If the bike pulls to one side (i.e. you need to put more force on one bar than the other to keep the bike in a straight line), then the frame could well be bent. The same goes if it appears to corner better in one direction than the other. There should be no wobbles or weaves, whether in a straight line at speed, or when cornering.

The headstock is a key place to look for crash damage, as this usually takes the full force of a front end impact. If the paint is flaking off here (but the rest of the frame paint is fine) then ask the owner why. Very early T595 Daytonas were suseptible to cracked frames at quite low speed collisions, but all the affected bikes were recalled by the factory and rebuilt into new frames – no problem has been heard of since.

With crash damage in mind, have a look round the whole bike for clues. Scrapes on the footrests could be just caused by enthusiastic riding, but anything more means the bike has been dropped. Are the crashbars damaged, or are they suspiciously new and shiny on an elderly bike, suggesting recent replacement? Ditto new mirrors, pannier rack or footrests. Are the handlebars straight and pointing in the right direction?

Finally, on the test ride, the bike should run straight and true when pointed down the road, without pulling to either side. It should go round corners without wobbles or weaves.

Stands 4 3 2 1

Many of the spine-frame bikes were fitted with a centre stand as well as a side stand, but it was an option on the injected bikes, and is most commonly found on the ST. It's a useful item for chain adjustment and lubing, though it adds a bit of weight.

Eventually the stand pivots will wear, so if the bike has a centre stand, heave the bike onto it and try twisting it from side to side – on firm ground, it shouldn't move. You're unlikely to find a stand this worn, as most owners will use the more convenient side stand day-to-day.

All Triumphs had a side stand, and it has a lot of weight to support, so check that it isn't loose or bent. The stands can bend if owners sat on the bike when it was supported only by the side stand – they weren't designed to take this weight, however slim the rider!

The bike should not wobble on the centre stand.

The side stand should be secure and straight.

Electrics 4 3 2 1

It used to be a cliché of motorcycling that old British bikes – and the old Triumphs were no exception – had unreliable electrics, but the new generation was determined to lay this to rest. And it did, because all the Hinckley Triumphs have reliable electrics, despite the complexity of the electronics on the later injected bikes. A new ECU, for example, is very expensive to replace, but they very rarely go wrong. Having said that, the ECU on the ST 1050 is quite vulnerable to crash damage, mounted

Check that everything works.

Headlight styles vary.

The rear/brake light can be overlooked.

Most wiring is out of sight. Watch for home-brewed modifications.

very close to the side of the fairing, on the left-hand side of the bike. If the machine you're looking at is being sold with damage on that side, check that the engine runs exactly as it should.

When looking over the seller's bike, you can't really take the tank off to check the state of the wiring, but you can check that absolutely everything electrical works as it should: lights, horn, indicators, all the warning lights and switchgear. If heated grips are fitted (standard on the Sprint ST from September 2003, and a popular option before then) check that they work on the test ride. If anything doesn't work, that's a good downward lever on the price.

With the engine idling, the alternator light should go out. If it doesn't, the alternator isn't charging. The alternator drive shaft bolts can fail on pre-2002 bikes, manifested by a rattle at idling speed. From 2002, bikes had a hollow drive shaft with a long through-bolt which cured the problem.

Ignition coils can fail at 20-30,000 miles, betrayed by misfiring, and the spine-frame four-cylinder bikes are more prone to this than the triples. They used twin double-ended coils, and the triples three single-ended coils. Misfiring may also be due to plug leads coming loose at the plug end, and on cruisers, with the engine more open to the elements, water can find its way down to the plugs, allowing them to rust into place over time – that's a rare problem though, as the cruiser Triumphs tend to be used on dry days only.

Another ignition problem is the ignition pick-up triggers. If the bike starts well from cold, dies after about 10 minutes, then is OK again after cooling down, this is likely to be the cause. The triggers are relatively cheap and easy to replace, though on faired bikes, the bodywork has to come off to gain access, and the connector underneath the carburettors on spine-frame machines is awkward to disconnect 'blind.'

Batteries are relatively easy to replace, but still an expense, and if the bike has been sitting unused over winters, the battery will have suffered, unless it was kept topped up with charge. It should have no problem spinning the big motor over from cold.

Wheels/tyres

All Hinckley Triumphs used cast alloy wheels, apart from the cruisers and the pre-2004 Tiger, which used spoked wheels with tubed tyres. On spoked wheels, check that none of the spokes are broken, bent or missing, though this is unlikely to be the case unless a bike has been badly neglected. But do also check that all the spokes are in tension – to check, tap each one with a screwdriver blade; a clear ring means they're nice and tight.

The following applies to all types of wheels. If the bike has a centre stand, put the bike on it and spin each wheel. It should run true, and there should be no dents or cracks in the rim.

Now check the wheel bearings. These aren't expensive, but fitting

A wheel bearing check is easy to do.

them is a hassle, and if there's play it could affect the handling. To check the front wheel, put the steering on full lock and try rocking the wheel in a vertical plane, then spin the wheel (only possible with a centre stand) and listen for rumbles. Give the rear wheel the same rocking and rumbling checks.

Tyre life varies wildly according to riding style, but all the Hinckley Triumphs are big, heavy bikes, so none of them are particularly light on tyres. Keen types who are heavy on the throttle

Check alloy rims for corrosion and dents.

Spoked wheels on Tiger and cruisers.

and brakes, and/or do a lot of high speed, heavily laden motorway miles, will wear down that rubber far quicker than a more gentle rider. Ask the seller for an indication, but steadier riders should get 6-7000 miles per tyre, front and rear. Harder riders on a sports tyre like a Continental Road Attack can expect 3000 miles rear, 3500 front.

The tyres should have a good 50 per cent of their tread left – if they have less, factor the replacement cost in when bargaining over the price. Check them over for

Less than 50 per cent remaining tread is a useful bargaining counter.

damage and sidewall cracks. Look at the wear pattern. Are they worn right round, or is the edge of the tread untouched by tarmac? The former suggests a hard rider (not necessarily a bad thing, so long as they've looked after the bike). Tyre brand is often down to personal choice, but Bridgestones are highly rated by some Triumph riders.

Steering head bearings   4   3   2   1

Like wheel bearings, steering head bearings don't cost an arm or leg, but trouble here can affect the handling, and changing them is a big job. With the bike on

the centre stand (if it has one), swing the handlebars from lock to lock. They should move freely, with not a hint of roughness or stiff patches – if there is, budget for replacing the bearings. To check for play, put the steering on full lock, grip the base of the forks and try rocking them back and forth.

If there is movement at the fork clamp, then the steering head bearings are loose – they may just need adjusting, but they're just as likely to be dented and need replacing. It's easy to confuse movement here with play in the fork sliders

The steering head bearing condition affects handling.

or stanchions – it might even be the centre stand wobbling! The bottom line is that movement of any sort here needs further investigation – whether you choose to bring in an expert, take the bike to a dealer or walk away from the whole deal is up to you. Or show the movement to the owner and use it as a bargaining tool. When testing the forks by pumping them up and down, a clonking sound or movement at the steering head again indicates that the bearings need attention.

Front forks   4   3   2   1

All Triumphs have conventional telescopic front forks, those on the spine-frame models supplied by either Kayaba or Showa. Both can suffer from oil leaks around the seals, but the Kayabas are more prone to this. You can tell them apart because the spring on the outside of the dust seal is visible on Showas, not on Kayabas. The fork stanchions

Check that the forks work smoothly.

Check forks for oil leaks – only early Tigers had gaiters.

Stanchions should be clean, rust-free and unpitted.

should be clean, and not pitted or rusted, and if that's the case, they should not leak.

Now check for wear. With the bike on its centre stand (if fitted) check for play in the forks by grasping the bottom of the legs and trying to rock the fork legs back and forth. As mentioned above, if you do detect movement, the next step is to find out where it's coming from. You should be able to see movement in the forks, if that's where the wear is. If there is no centre stand, see you if you can detect play while pumping the forks up and down, in test below.

The forks should also be parallel – that is, appear to be in the same plane when viewed from the side. If they're not, they may have been twisted after hitting something. Take the bike off the centre stand, hold the front brake on and pump the forks up and down: they should move through their whole travel smoothly and freely with no squeaks or rattles.

The only Triumphs fitted with fork gaiters as standard were the 885 and 955cc Tigers (i.e. up to October 2006). These should be firmly in place and in good condition, with no tears. Nice looking gaiters can hide leaky forks, and to check for this, grasp the gaiter and rub it against the fork tube: it should resist movement, but if it slides easily, the chances are that the fork leg is oily because the seal is leaking. Check both forks in this way – if one gaiter slides more easily than the other, you can be sure there's a problem.

Rear suspension

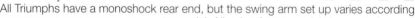

All Triumphs have a monoshock rear end, but the swing arm set up varies according

to model. All spine-frame models have a twin-sided swing arm, as does the injected Sprint RS and Tiger. All others (including a special edition Sprint RS from September 2003) have a single-sided swing arm, the pivot of which can seize up if neglected. The rear suspension linkages on all bikes should have been lubricated every three years – ask the owner when this was last done,

Single-sided swing arm fitted to many fuel-injected bikes.

though linkage wear doesn't appear to be a particular problem. Get down on the ground and have a look at them – do they look clean and well lubed, or caked in mud and neglected?

On the test ride, seek out the odd manhole cover or pothole – if the suspension feels oversoft and bouncy, then the rear shock may need replacing. Do make sure that the spring pre-load is adjusted properly for your weight, though the seller may not want you to adjust the shock away from his preferred settings.

The shock should not be bouncy or oversoft.

Chain/sprockets

④ ③ ② ①

With the engine switched off, examine the final drive chain and sprockets. Is the chain clean, well lubed and properly adjusted? The best way to check how worn it is is to take hold of a link and try to pull it rearwards away from the sprocket. It should only reveal a small portion of the sprocket teeth – any more, and it needs replacing.

Check the rear sprocket teeth for wear – if they have a hooked appearance, the sprocket needs replacing. Ditto if any teeth are damaged or missing. And if the rear sprocket needs replacing, then the gearbox sprocket will too. The chain and sprockets aren't massively expensive, but changing the gearbox sprocket takes some dismantling time.

Does the chain look well cared for?

Worn sprockets are a good bargaining counter.

Clutch

④ ③ ② ①

As with tyres, ultimate clutch life depends on riding style, and an abusive rider can wear out any clutch in short order. However, Triumph clutches are very strong, not prone to slip or drag, and the author came across one 240,000-mile Trident with the original clutch. Speed Triples, by their nature, are more likely to have had a hard clutch life than, say, a Thunderbird or Sprint ST.

All are cable operated, so a jerky or heavy operation could be just down to an old or unlubricated cable. Check that the cable has the correct small amount of free play.

The clutch cable should operate smoothly.

Gearbox

More good news. As with the clutch, Triumph gearboxes are tough and long-lasting. Early T595 Daytonas were occasionally troubled by fourth gear breaking up, and

Early gearboxes are a little clunky, later ones quieter.

Gearbox failures like this are very rare.

if any bike was affected, this should have been cured by now. Generally, though, gearboxes only give trouble if they are allowed to run short of oil, or if the bike has been raced – spine-frame Speed Triples may have taken part in the Triumph-sponsored Speed Triple Challenge. That will show up in a noisy gearbox with a tendency to slip out of gear.

Spine-frame gearboxes are noisier than later units, and first gear engages with a definite clunk, but that's inherent, and not a sign of trouble. Later boxes engage more quietly and smoothly – the Sprint ST 1050 has looser-fitting gearbox dogs, which enable a more gradual engagement.

Instruments/switchgear

Triumphs used a variety of instruments, but the general pattern is analogue dials on the spine-frame bikes, and an analogue rev counter with digital speedo on all the injected bikes (apart from the pre-November 2004 Sprint ST and Tiger, which had a full set of conventional dials, including fuel and temp gauges). Rev counters are electronic, rather than cable-driven, and all bikes had one. On the test ride, check that all these various instruments work, and the same goes for the warning lights – oil pressure, main beam, indicators, alternator, etc.

Minimal instrumentation on the Sprint RS.

Nearly all early spine-frames had the same instrument set.

Check that all switchgear works.

Triumph switchgear is industry-standard stuff, identical to that used on many Japanese and European bikes. It's very reliable, with no particular problems, and if an over-enthusiastic jet wash does force water into a switch, a good squirt of WD-40 should get it working again.

Cables

All the control cables – throttle, choke (if fitted), clutch – should work smoothly without stiffness or jerking. Poorly lubricated, badly adjusted cables are an indication of general neglect, and the same goes for badly routed cables.

Cables (clutch and throttle) should be unfrayed and well lubed.

Engine – general impression

The good news is that by motorcycle standards the Triumph triples and fours are tremendously robust engines, and they can be very long-lived indeed. The bottom end is virtually unburstable, and there are some bikes around with over 100,000 or even 200,000 miles on the original engine, given no more than routine maintenance.

That said, Triumph engines need to be looked after, like any other piece of engineering, and the secret to long life appears to be regular oil/filter changes – the recommended interval is 6000 miles – which probably are of greater benefit than spending a lot of money on synthetic oil. Other key maintenance points are a valve clearance check every 12,000 miles and (on spine-frame bikes) a carburettor balance every 6000.

A tatty exterior appearance doesn't necessarily mean internal neglect, but watch out for chewed up fasteners where someone's tried to use the wrong size of Allen key. On spine-frame bikes, look for fuel leaks around the carbs. And on all bikes (though this is easier on those without a fairing) check the condition of the various coolant hoses – any that are cracked will need replacing.

Engines can run to high mileages with just routine maintenance.

While we're talking cooling system, the radiator should be reasonably clear of mud and crud.

Ideally, the bike will have a full service history at a Triumph franchise dealer or a specialist, though that might be asking a bit much of a low-priced 18-year-old Trident 900. In any case, these engines can also stand up if the official maintenance schedule isn't strictly

Check coolant hoses for cracks and bulging.

adhered to. The author came across one tatty looking Daytona 900 with 89,000 miles showing – for the previous 70,000, it had not had the carbs balanced or tappets checked, yet it ran fine and sounded healthy.

Engine – starting/running

The engine should start promptly and idle smoothly, whether it's a carburettor unit in a spine-frame, or an injected one. Any fuelling problems on a fuel-injected bike are a job for a Triumph dealer, because they have the diagnostic equipment.

Start up – there shouldn't be a problem.

However, starting can be one of the very few persistent problems that affects Hinckley Triumphs. The starter sprag clutch is a one-way clutch which allows the starter to engage. If the sprag only engages partially, it starts to wear the clutch teeth away until eventually it fails altogether. It's often caused by attempting to start the engine with a weak battery. Change the battery every three years (and keep it topped off if the bike is stored over the winter) and this shouldn't be a problem.

Another tip from mechanically sympathetic owners is not to press the starter a second time until the engine had stopped spinning from the first attempt – this also gives the sprag clutch an easier time.

If the sprag clutch has failed on the bike you're looking at, it should be obvious. The starter will either fail to engage at all, and whirr over at high speed, or clunk noisily as it tries to mesh. That said, the real test is when the engine

2002-on bikes with this clutch cover have a more easily accessible sprag clutch.

is cold – a sprag clutch that works fine when the engine is warm may fail to do its job from cold. So if possible, test start a cold engine.

The starter sprag clutch can be a big job to replace.

For pre-1994 bikes, changing the sprag clutch was a relatively easy job that took 1.5 hours, thanks to an access lid into the crankcase, situated underneath the carburettors. From 1994, Triumph increased the sprag clutch teeth from 51 to 53, assumed this had cured the problem and deleted the access lid. Unfortunately it didn't cure it, and changing a sprag on 1994-2001 bikes involves removing the engine and splitting the crankcases, which can turn into a 1.5 day job, say

x500 plus parts for a franchise dealer. The sprag itself costs around x70.

The situation was improved in October 2001, when the sprag clutch was moved to the end of the crankshaft, where it is easier and quicker to change. Failure also became much less common, though it can still happen. The easiest way to tell these later bikes apart from the earlier ones is the appearance of the right-hand crankcase (though it's easier on naked bikes than those with fairings). Spine-frame bikes had a large clutch cover with the Triumph logo cast into it; pre-2002 injected bikes had a smaller rounded cover, and post-2002 the cover was smaller still, with three Allen bolts. For the 1050 from November 2004, the style changed again, to a bigger clutch cover. Identification is easy with the Sprint RS: pre-2002, silver engine; 2002-on, black engine.

The sprag clutch isn't a fatal Achilles heel, so don't let this one potential fault put you off Triumphs altogether, and some bikes are completely unaffected by it – the 240,000-mile Trident mentioned earlier had its sprag clutch changed only once.

Engine – smoke/noise

If you're used to ultra-quiet modern bikes, then a spine-frame Triumph can come as a bit of a shock. These early engines are mechanically quite noisy, with a large amount of rustle and whirr from the unit. Hinckley made great efforts to quieten the later engines, such as making the balancer shaft drive gears quieter, and that bore fruit. The important point is that this mechanical noise is inherent, and nothing to worry about.

Blip the throttle and watch for blue smoke.

Don't be surprised by rustles and whirrs at idle on spine-frame engines.

Later triples, like this 1050, are mechanically quieter.

That said, you do need to be aware of rattles and clatters that are signs of trouble. As mentioned before, these motors are extremely robust, and it's most unlikely that you will find one suffering from bearing knock or pumping out blue smoke, but it's worth being beware of known potential faults.

A clatter at idle on the four-cylinder machines can result from the balance shafts being out of adjustment. Excess slack in the drive gears should be adjusted out at service time, and it is a straightforward job after the fairing has been removed for access. As mentioned, pre-2002 bikes can suffer

On four-cylinder engines, a rattle at idle may be the balance shafts out of adjustment.

from a sheared bolt on the alternator drive shaft, and this manifests itself as a rattle when the engine is idling. Again, a fairly straightforward job to fix, but any fairing panels have to be removed first.

As with any chain-driven overhead cam engine, the cam chain and its tensioner are important components for the unit's health. The Triumph items aren't prone to problems, but one specialist recommends that the cam chain should be changed at 24,000 miles in any case, as it will eventually stretch and become too slack for the tensioner to do its job.

Unlike an oil-cooled BMW twin, which may use quite a lot of oil until it has broken in, Triumphs should not be great consumers of oil, with no more than minor top-ups between changes. As with any engine, poor oil consumption and blue smoke are a sign of cylinder bore and valve guide wear, though they don't appear to be prone to this.

If the cooling system is in good condition, the engine should not use a drop of coolant. Some early bikes didn't have sealant at the base of the cylinder liner, the idea being that torquing the cylinder head down would be sufficient to ensure a water-tight seal. It wasn't, and can lead to a very slight but constant coolant loss into the oil – not enough to show in the lubricant, but enough to require topping-up every now and then.

Brakes ④ ③ ② ①

On 21st century bikes, we're used to effortless two-finger stopping, and often

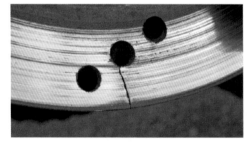

Examine discs for cracks.

ABS as well. The spine-frame Triumphs had solid discs and two-piston calipers, which were just about adequate for a 220kg bike capable of 130mph, and by modern standards these early brakes are not strong, even when in tip-top condition. It's something worth bearing in mind if you've just stepped off a modern bike, and you should ride accordingly. The exception is the rare Daytona Super III, which used Triumph's own six-pot front calipers and had very good brakes.

Things improved with the fuel-injected bikes, which use four-pot Nissin floating calipers. These are very good and well up to contemporary standards, which includes the 1997-

Later front brakes, with four-pot calipers, are very good.

An underslung rear caliper is vulnerable to sticking.

Brake hoses must be free of cracks and kinks.

on T595 Daytona with Nissin calipers and twin 320mm front discs.

However, all of these brakes need to be checked for sticking pads. If the bike doesn't roll freely as you push it, then it's likely that the calipers need a strip down and clean. Neglect here can reach a point where a new or good secondhand caliper is the only answer. Pad plates should always be coated with anti-seize compound whenever they're removed, and any competent owner or dealer will have done this. The underslung rear caliper of spine-frame Daytonas and all Speed Triples is particularly prone to sticking, either because of its vulnerable position to road dirt, or because its out of sight nature means it can get forgotten.

Otherwise, all the usual brake items apply: check for fluid leaks from the master cylinder, the pad thickness and the disc for thickness, cracks or a worn lip on the outer extremity. The brake fluid should be clear, not cloudy. Also check the brake

hoses for cracks, kinks or leaks. With an assistant holding the brakes on, check that the hoses aren't bulging. (This doesn't apply to later bikes fitted with braided hose.) An early bike with braided hose is a sign of a conscientious owner.

ABS is an option on the 1050 Sprint ST and Tiger. It's probably not a good idea to check whether this is working when on the test ride, but you *can* note whether the ABS warning light goes out, as it should. If there's any doubt about the ABS system, repairing it is a dealer job.

Exhaust

A rotten exhaust, whether it's downpipes or silencers that need replacing, is a major expense, but, fortunately, Triumph exhausts seem to last

Downpipes last well – these have just lost some paint.

A shiny silencer can hide a rotted interior.

very well. It's not unusual to see a 50,000-mile bike with the original system still in good condition.

Remember that shiny chrome can hide rotten internals, so blip the throttle and listen to the engine – it shouldn't be excessively noisy, and, if it has recently passed a roadworthiness test (the MoT in the UK), then so much the better.

Watch for 'off-road use only' silencers, which could be official Triumph cans or aftermarket items. These are more likely to be found on Daytonas and Speed Triples – lots of riders fit them, but strictly speaking they are illegal for road use and could invalidate your insurance. A quality stainless steel aftermarket system is a sign of an owner prepared to invest in the bike.

Luggage   4️⃣ 3️⃣ 2️⃣ 1️⃣

If looking at a Trophy, Tiger or Sprint ST, it is highly likely to have decent quality hard luggage fitted. Owners of these bikes tend to take them touring, and are prepared to spend money on proper luggage. This is often Triumph's own cases, and factory panniers were fitted as standard to 2004-on Sprint ST's and Tigers. Colour-matched to the bike, they undoubtedly increase a bike's value as well as its usefulness.

Check panniers outside for damage and inside for water ingress.

Many STs have a topbox as well as panniers.

Check the panniers for scuff marks and missing badges, that the locks work smoothly and allow the panniers to be removed/replaced easily. Open them up and check for water ingress – they should be waterproof. Triumph's panniers are generally well made and keep luggage dry, though early Sprint ST 1050 cases were made of thinner plastic, allowing them to distort when fully loaded and let water in. These cases should have been recalled and replaced with double-skinned items, which cured the problem.

Test ride

However carefully you examine the bike and listen to the engine, there's no substitute for a test ride to get a real feel for what sort of condition it's in. This should be not less than 15 minutes, and you should be doing the riding – not the seller riding with you on the pillion. It's understandable that some sellers are reluctant to let a complete stranger loose on their pride and joy, but it does go with the territory of selling a bike, and so long as you leave an article of faith (usually the vehicle you arrived in) then all should be happy. Take your driving licence in case the seller wants to see it.

The bike should start promptly, after which you should give yourself a short while to familiarise yourself with the controls, tug at the levers and blip the throttle, to get a feel for the bike. Check that oil and ignition lights have gone out, select first gear (which should click in easily) and set off – clutch take-up should be smooth and progressive.

All Triumph triples and fours (with the exception of the 750s and Daytona 1000) are torquey engines with a very strong midrange, so the bike should accelerate briskly in all gears and respond instantly with no hiccups or hesitation. While accelerating, check the clutch isn't slipping.

Spine-frame Triumphs are not Yamaha R1s, and the handling is best described as stable rather than flickable, but the bike should turn in cleanly as soon as you nudge the bars, and track well through any corner, with no wobbling. Fuel-injected bikes are significantly lighter and more nimble. Whatever the model, it should brake smoothly and progressively, though as noted above, early brakes aren't up to modern standards. Towards the end of the test ride, if you haven't tried one of these bikes before, think beyond the condition, and whether you would be happy owning and riding it: does it fit you? Is it comfortable and does the rough-edged character of the original triple appeal?

Back at base, check that the engine settles back into a nice steady idle before switching off. If all is well, talk to the owner about price. If you've discovered a fault, and he/she won't make a deal, then thank the owner for their time and walk away.

Evaluation procedure
Add up the total points.
Score: 100 = excellent; 75 = good; 50 = average; 25 = poor.

Bikes scoring over 70 will be completely usable and will require only maintenance and care to preserve condition. Bikes scoring between 25 and 51 will require serious restoration (at much the same cost regardless of score). Bikes scoring between 52 and 69 will require very careful assessment of necessary repair/restoration costs in order to arrive at a realistic value.

10 Auctions
– sold! Another way to buy your dream

Auction pros & cons
Pros: Prices will usually be lower than those of dealers or private sellers and you might grab a real bargain on the day. Auctioneers have usually established clear title with the seller. At the venue you can usually examine documentation relating to the bike.

Cons: You have to rely on a sketchy catalogue description of condition and history. The opportunity to inspect is limited and you cannot ride the bike. Auction machines can be a little below par and may require some work. It's easy to overbid. There will usually be a buyer's premium to pay in addition to the auction hammer price.

Which auction?
Auctions by established auctioneers are advertised in the motorcycle magazines and on the auction houses' websites. A catalogue, or a simple printed list of the lots for auctions might only be available a day or two ahead, though often lots are listed and pictured on auctioneers' websites much earlier. Contact the auction company to ask if previous auction selling prices are available as this is useful information (details of past sales are often available on websites).

Catalogue, entry fee and payment details
When you purchase the catalogue of the bikes in the auction, it often acts as a ticket allowing two people to attend the viewing days and the auction. Catalogue details tend to be comparatively brief, but will include information such as 'one owner from new, low mileage, full service history', etc. It will also usually show a guide price to give you some idea of what to expect to pay and will tell you what is charged as a 'Buyer's premium'. The catalogue will also contain details of acceptable forms of payment. At the fall of the hammer an immediate deposit is usually required, the balance payable within 24 hours. If the plan is to pay by cash there may be a cash limit. Some auctions will accept payment by debit card. Sometimes credit or charge cards are acceptable, but will often incur an extra charge. A bank draft or bank transfer will have to be arranged in advance with your own bank as well as with the auction house. No bike will be released before all payments are cleared. If delays occur in payment transfers then storage costs can accrue.

Buyer's premium
A buyer's premium will be added to the hammer price: don't forget this in your calculations. It is not usual for there to be a further state tax or local tax on the purchase price and/or on the buyer's premium.

Viewing
In some instances it's possible to view on the day, or days before, as well as in the hours prior to, the auction. There are auction officials available who are willing to help out if need be. While the officials may start the engine for you, a test ride is

out of the question. Crawling under and around the bike as much as you want is permitted. You can also ask to see any documentation available.

Bidding
Before you take part in the auction, decide your maximum bid - and stick to it!

It may take a while for the auctioneer to reach the lot you are interested in, so use that time to observe how other bidders behave. When it's the turn of your bike, attract the auctioneer's attention and make an early bid. The auctioneer will then look to you for a reaction every time another bid is made. Usually the bids will be in fixed increments until the bidding slows, when smaller increments will often be accepted before the hammer falls. If you want to withdraw from the bidding, make sure the auctioneer understands your intentions - a vigorous shake of the head when he or she looks to you for the next bid should do the trick!

Assuming that you are the successful bidder, the auctioneer will note your card or paddle number, and from that moment on you will be responsible for the bike.

If it is unsold, either because it failed to reach the reserve or because there was little interest, it may be possible to negotiate with the owner, via the auctioneers, after the sale is over.

Successful bid
There are two more items to think about - how to get the bike home, and insurance. If you can't ride it, your own or a hired trailer is one way, another is to have it shipped using the facilities of a local company. The auction house will also have details of companies specialising in the transport of bikes.
Insurance for immediate cover can usually be purchased on site, but it may be more cost-effective to make arrangements with your own insurance company in advance, and then call to confirm the full details.

eBay & other online auctions?
eBay & other online auctions could land you a Triumph at a bargain price, though you'd be foolhardy to bid without examining it first, something most vendors encourage. A useful feature of eBay is that the geographical location of the bike is shown, so you can narrow your choices to those within a realistic radius of home. Be prepared to be outbid in the last few moments of the auction. Remember, your bid is binding and that it will be very, very difficult to get restitution in the case of a crooked vendor fleecing you – caveat emptor!

Be aware that some bikes offered for sale in online auctions are 'ghost' machines. Don't part with any cash without being sure that the vehicle does actually exist and is as described (usually pre-bidding inspection is possible).

Auctioneers
Bonhams	www.bonhams.com
British Car Auctions (BCA)	www.bca-europe.com or www.british-car-auctions.co.uk
Cheffins	www.cheffins.co.uk
DVCA	www.dvca.co.uk
eBay	www.ebay.com
H&H	www.classic-auctions.co.uk
Shannons	www.shannons.com.au
Silver	www.silverauctions.com

11 Paperwork

– correct documentation is essential!

The paper trail

Classic bikes sometimes come with a large portfolio of paperwork accumulated and passed on by a succession of proud owners. This documentation represents the real history of the machine, from which you can deduce how well it's been cared for, how much it's been used, which specialists have worked on it, and the dates of major repairs and restorations. All of this information will be priceless to you as the new owner, so be very wary of bikes with little paperwork to support their claimed history.

Registration documents

All countries/states have some form of registration for private vehicles, whether it's like the American 'pink slip' system or the British 'log book' system.

It is essential to check that the registration document is genuine, that it relates to the bike in question, and that all the details are correctly recorded, including frame and engine numbers (if these are shown). If you are buying from the previous owner, his or her name and address will be recorded in the document: this will not usually be the case if you are buying from a dealer.

In the UK the current (Euro-aligned) registration document is the V5C, and is printed in coloured sections of blue, green and pink. The blue section relates to the motorcycle specification, the green section has details of the registered keeper (who is not necessarily the legal owner) and the pink section is sent to the DVLA in the UK when the bike is sold. A small section in yellow deals with selling within the motor trade.

In the UK the DVLA will provide details of earlier keepers of the bike upon payment of a small fee, and much can be learned in this way.

If the bike has a foreign registration there may be expensive and time-consuming formalities to complete. Do you really want the hassle? Importing a bike from the USA for example involves a 6% import duty and 17.5% VAT as well as the cost of shipping and paperwork. In the UK, such a wide choice of Triumphs are available, that this is unlikely to be worthwhile, but buyers in other countries looking for something rare (such as a Daytona Super III or 1200) might well find it worth importing a bike from Britain.

Roadworthiness certificate

Most country/state administrations require that bikes are regularly tested to prove that they are safe to use on the public highway. In the UK that test (the 'MoT') is carried out at approved testing stations, for a fee. In the USA the requirement varies, but most states insist on an emissions test every two years as a minimum, whilst the police are charged with pulling over unsafe-looking vehicles.

In the UK the test is required on an annual basis for any bike over three years old. Of particular relevance for older bikes is that the certificate issued includes the mileage reading recorded at the test date and, therefore, becomes an independent record of that machine's history. Ask the seller if previous certificates are available. Without an MoT the vehicle should be trailered to its new home, unless you insist that a valid MoT is part of the deal. (Not such a bad idea this, as at least you will know the bike was roadworthy on the day it was tested and you don't need to wait for the old certificate to expire before having the test done.)

Road licence
The administration of every country/state charges some kind of tax for the use of its road system, the actual form of the 'road licence' and, how it is displayed, varying enormously country to country and state to state.

Whatever the form of the road licence, it must relate to the vehicle carrying it and must be present and valid if the bike is to be ridden on the public highway legally. The value of the licence will depend on the length of time it will continue to be valid.

In the UK if a bike is untaxed because it has not been used for a period of time, the owner has to inform the licencing authorities, otherwise the vehicle's date-related registration number will be lost and there will be a painful amount of paperwork to get it re-registered. Also in the UK, bikes built before the end of 1972 are exempt from road tax, though this obviously doesn't apply to any of the Hinckley Triumphs.

Certificates of authenticity
For many makes of classic bike it is possible to get a certificate proving the age and authenticity (e.g. engine and frame numbers, paint colour and trim) of a particular machine. These are sometimes called 'Heritage Certificates' and if the bike comes with one of these it is a definite bonus. If you want to obtain one, the owners club is the best starting point.

Valuation certificate
Hopefully, the vendor will have a recent valuation certificate, or letter signed by a recognised expert stating how much he, or she, believes the particular bike to be worth (such documents, together with photos, are usually needed to get 'agreed value' insurance). Generally such documents should act only as confirmation of your own assessment of the bike rather than a guarantee of value as the expert has probably not seen it in the flesh. The easiest way to find out how to obtain a formal valuation is to contact the owners club.

Service history
Older Hinckley Triumphs are as likely to have been serviced at home by enthusiastic (and hopefully capable) owners, as they have by an official dealer. Nevertheless, try to obtain as much service history and other paperwork pertaining to the bike as you can. Naturally official dealer receipts score most points in the value stakes. However, anything helps in the great authenticity game, items like the original bill of sale, handbook, parts invoices and repair bills, adding to the story and the character of the machine. Even a brochure correct to the year of the bike's manufacture is a useful document and something that you could well have to search hard to locate in future years. If the seller claims that the bike has been restored, then expect receipts and other evidence from a specialist restorer.

If the seller claims to have carried out regular servicing, ask what work was completed, when, and seek some evidence of it being carried out. Your assessment of the bike's overall condition should tell you whether the seller's claims are genuine.

12 What's it worth to you?
– let your head rule your heart!

Condition

If the bike you've been looking at is really ratty, then you've probably not bothered to use the marking system in chapter 9 – 30 minute evaluation. You may not have even got as far as using that chapter at all!

If you did use the marking system in chapter 9 you'll know whether the bike is in Excellent (maybe Concours), Good, Average or Poor condition or, perhaps, somewhere in between these categories.

To keep up to date with prices, buy the latest editions of the bike magazines (also *Bike Trader* and *MCN* in the UK) and check the classified and dealer ads – these are particularly useful as they enable you to compare private and dealer prices. Also check whether your national Triumph club has a 'bikes for sale' section – this may only be open to members, but if you're serious about buying a Hinckley bike it'll be worth joining anyway.

Hinckley Triumphs are relatively modern machines, and there are a lot of them around, so the usual rules about buying a classic bike as an investment don't apply (with the possible exception of the rarer special editions, such as the Daytona Super III, 1200 SE and Speed Triple 750). Early spine-frames are still the cheapest bikes to buy, and the actual price reflects condition and mileage rather than age. Prices are unlikely to fall much further, and these bikes come up for sale far less frequently than the fuel-injected ones.

Depreciation will affect the fuel-injected bikes though, as they are newer machines in plentiful supply, and this situation is likely to continue for some time – at the time of writing, the Sprint ST, Tiger and Speed Triple 1050 are selling in reasonable numbers, so more are coming onto the secondhand market all the time.

Before you start haggling with the seller, consider what effect any variation from standard specification might have on the bike's value. This is a personal thing: for some, absolute originality is non-negotiable, while others see non-standard parts as an opportunity to pick up a bargain. Practical extras such as quality hard luggage and heated grips will actually increase the bike's value. If you are buying from a dealer, remember there will be a dealer's premium on the price.

Striking a deal

Negotiate on the basis of your condition assessment, mileage, and fault rectification cost. Also take into account the bike's specification. Be realistic about the value, but don't be completely intractable: a small compromise on the part of the vendor or buyer will often facilitate a deal at little real cost.

13 Do you really want to restore?

– it'll take longer and cost more than you think ...

Do you really want to restore?

There's a romance attached to restoration projects; about bringing a sick bike back to blooming health, and it's tempting to buy something that 'just needs a few small jobs' to bring it up to scratch. But there are two things to think about here. One; once you've got the bike home and start taking it apart, those few small jobs could turn into big ones. Two; restoration takes time, which is a precious thing in itself. Be honest with yourself – will you get as much pleasure from working on the bike as you will from riding it?

This applies to restoring any bike, but in the case of a Hinckley Triumph, you need to think harder still. The plain fact is that these bikes are too numerous, and not yet old enough, to be classed as an investment. There's no doubt that the triple in all its guises is a design classic, but that hasn't translated into appreciating values just yet. So if you do buy a cheap and tatty bike, its increased value as a result of your restoration is unlikely to justify the time and money spent on it.

Restoring a Triumph yourself requires a number of skills, which is fine if you already have them, but if you haven't it's good not to make your newly acquired bike part of the learning curve! Can you weld? Are you confident about building up an engine? Do you have a warm, well-lit garage with a solid workbench and a good selection of tools?

A rolling restoration is tempting, especially as the summer begins to pass with your bike still off the road. This is not the way to achieve a concours finish, which can only really be achieved via a thorough nut-and-bolt rebuild, without the bike getting wet, gritty and salty in the meantime. But there's a lot to be said for a rolling restoration. Riding the bike helps maintain your interest as its condition improves, and it's also more affordable than trying to do everything in one go. In the long run, it will take longer, but you'll get some on-road fun out of the bike in the meantime.

But maybe the bottom line is this. There are lots of Triumphs around, and they are not (yet) collector's items, making a home restoration even less worthwhile. Better to buy a bike that's ready to ride, and enjoy it ...

Buying a usable bike, as opposed to a restoration project, may prove cheaper in the long run.

14 Paint faults
– a bad complexion, including dimples. pimples, and bubbles

Paint faults generally occur due to lack of protection/maintenance, or to poor preparation prior to a respray or touch-up. Some of the following conditions may be present in the bike you're looking at:

Orange peel
This appears as an uneven paint surface, similar to the appearance of the skin of an orange. The fault is caused by the failure of atomised paint droplets to flow into each other when they hit the surface. It's sometimes possible to rub out the effect with proprietary paint cutting/rubbing compound or very fine grades of abrasive paper. A respray may be necessary in severe cases. Consult a paint shop for advice.

Minor scratches can often be polished out ...

Cracking
Severe cases are likely to have been caused by too heavy an application of paint (or filler beneath the paint). Also, insufficient stirring of the paint before application can lead to the components being improperly mixed, and cracking can result. Incompatibility with the paint already on the panel can have a similar effect. To rectify it is necessary to rub down to a smooth, sound finish before respraying the problem area.

Crazing
Sometimes the paint takes on a crazed rather than a cracked appearance when the problems mentioned under 'cracking' are present. This problem can also be caused by a reaction between the underlying surface and the paint. Paint removal and respraying the problem area is usually the only solution.

... though sometimes there's no choice but to respray.

Blistering
Almost always caused by corrosion of the metal beneath the paint. Usually perforation will be found in the metal and the damage will usually be worse than that suggested by the area of blistering. The metal will have to be repaired before repainting.

Micro blistering
Usually the result of an economy respray where inadequate heating has allowed moisture to settle on the vehicle before spraying. Consult a paint specialist, but

damaged paint will have to be removed before partial or full respraying. Can also be caused by bike covers that don't 'breathe.'

Fading
Some colours, especially reds, are prone to fading if subject to strong sunlight for long periods without the benefit of polish protection. Sometimes proprietary paint restorers and/or paint cutting/rubbing compunds will retrieve the situation. Often a respray is the only real solution.

Peeling
Often a problem with metallic paintwork when the sealing lacquer becomes damaged and begins to peel off. Poorly applied paint may also peel. The remedy is to strip and start again.

Dimples
Dimples in the paintwork are caused by the residue of polish (particularly silicone types) not being removed properly before respaying. Paint removal and repainting is the only solution.

A quality respray makes a good bike better.

Alloy corrodes over time – this is an extreme example.

Calipers will seize after months of inactivity, especially if the bike is parked outdoors.

Like any piece of engineering, and, indeed, like human beings, Hinckley Triumphs deteriorate if they sit doing nothing for long periods. This is especially relevant if the bike is laid up for six months of the year, as some are.

Rust
If the bike is put away wet, and/or stored in a cold, damp garage, the paint, metal and brightwork will suffer. Ensure the machine is completely dry and clean before going into storage, and if you can afford it, invest in a dehumidifier to keep the garage atmosphere dry.

Seized components
Pistons in brake calipers can seize partially or fully, resulting in binding or non-working brakes. Cables are vulnerable to seizure, too – the answer is to thoroughly lube them beforehand, and to give them a couple of pulls once a week or so.

Tyres
If the bike has been left on its side stand, most of its weight is on the tyres, which will subsequently develop

Tyres will crack and go hard if unused for a long time.

flat spots and cracks over time. Always leave the bike on its centre stand, if it has one, as this takes weight off the tyres. If there is no centre stand, move the bike a foot or so once a week. A paddock stand will keep the rear tyre clear of the ground.

Engine
Old, acidic oil can corrode bearings. Many riders change the oil in the spring, when they're putting the bike back on the road, but really it should be changed just before the bike is laid up, so that the bearings are sitting in fresh oil. When giving the cables their weekly exercise, don't start the engine – running it for a short time does more harm than good, as it produces a lot of moisture internally, which the engine doesn't get hot enough to burn off. That will attack the engine internals, and the silencers.

Battery/electrics
Either remove the battery and give it a top-up charge every couple of weeks, or connect it up to a battery top-up device such as the Optimate, which will keep it permanently fully charged. Damp conditions will allow fuses and earth connections to corrode, storing up electrical troubles for the spring. Eventually, wiring insulation will harden and fail.

Auctioneers

Bonhams
www.bonhams.com

British Car Auctions (BCA)
www.bca-europe.com or
www.british-car-auctions.co.uk

Cheffins
www.cheffins.co.uk

Dorset Vintage & Classic Auctions
http://www.dvca.co.uk

eBay
www.ebay.com

H&H
www.classic-auctions.co.uk

Shannons
www.shannons.com.au

Silver
www.silverauctions.com

Useful websites and clubs across the world

Triumph official website
www.triumph.co.uk
Tel: 01455 251700
National sites for USA, Canada,
Australia, New Zealand, France,
Germany, Austria, Spain and other
countries

Triumph Owners Club
www.tomcc.org
The original Triumph club, catering for
old-generation Triumphs as well as the
Hinckley bikes.

Riders Association of Triumph (RAT)
www.triumph.co.uk/uk/RAThome

The official club, open to all owners of
Hinckley Triumphs.

Triumph Owners Club – Germany
www.tomc.de

Triumph Owners Club – Sweden
www.tomccsweden.se
TOMCC Sweden, Box 5010, 514 05
Länghem

Triumph Owners Club – Norway
www.gmx.no/tomccn

Triumph Owners Club – Netherlands
www.triumphownersclub.nl

Triumph Riders Club – Netherlands
www.triumphriders.nl

Triumph Owners Club – Hungary
www.triumphclub.extra.hu

Triumph Tiger Club – Switzerland
www.tiger-club.ch

Triumph Tiger Owners Club
www.bikersoracle.com/tiger
Web-based club for all Tigers.

Tiger Triple
www.tigertriple.com
Forum for Tigers only.

Tiger 1050
www.tiger1050.com
Forum and information, devoted to the
Tiger 1050.

Triumph.net
www.triumphnet.com
Independent site for Sprint ST and RS
only. Lots of information.

T595.net
www.t595.net
Independent forum, established 1999, for all Hinckley Triumphs.

T5net Forum
www.t5net-forum.de
German forum for all Hinckley Triumphs.

RAT Yak
www.ratyak.com
Chat forum for RAT members.

Triumph Talk
www.triumphtalk.com

Triumph RAT
www.triumphrat.net
On-line forum.

Triumph specialists (UK)
The nearest Triumph specialist is most likely to be an official Triumph dealer. For location, go to the official Triumph website – www.triumph.co.uk. There are very few independents that specialise in Hinckley Triumphs, but for secondhand parts, try any of the general motorcycle breakers as well as the specialists listed below.

Sprint Manufacturing
www.triumphparts.co.uk
Tel: 01985 850821
Specialist in new and secondhand parts/accessories for Hinckley Triumphs.

Triumph Online
www.triumph-online.co.uk
Service spares and accessories.

Triumph-ant
www.triumph-ant.co.uk 01443 691666
New and secondhand spares, South Wales. Reconditioned engines.

Norman Hyde
www.normanhyde.co.uk
Mostly old-generation Triumphs, but also some accessories/upgrades for the Thunderbird.

17 Vital statistics
– essential data at your fingertips

To list the specification of every Hinckley Triumph would take up more room than we have, so here are three representative bikes: 1993 Trident 900, 2000 Tiger 900 and 2009 Sprint ST 1050.

Engine
1993 Trident 900: Liquid-cooled three-cylinder, DOHC, bore x stroke 76 x 65mm, capacity 885cc, compression ratio 10.6:1, max power 100PS @ 9000rpm, max torque 61lb ft @ 6500rpm
2000 Tiger: Liquid-cooled three-cylinder, fuel-injected, DOHC, bore x stroke 76 x 65mm, capacity 885cc, compression ratio 11.3:1, max power 86hp @ 8200rpm, max torque 62lb ft @ 6400rpm
2009 Sprint ST 1050: Liquid-cooled three-cylinder, fuel-injected, DOHC, bore x stroke 79 x 71.4mm, capacity 1050cc, compression ratio 12.0:1, max power 127PS @ 9250rpm, 77lb ft @ 7500rpm

Transmission
1993 Trident 900: 6-speed, ratios 2.73, 1.947, 1.545, 1.291, 1.154, 1.074:1
2000 Tiger 900: 6-speed, ratios 2.73, 1.947, 1.545, 1.291, 1.154, 1.074:1
2009 Sprint ST 1050: 6-speed

Brakes
1993 Trident 900: Front 2 x 296cc discs, 2-pot calipers, rear 1 x 255mm disc, 2-pot caliper
2000 Tiger 900: Front 2 x 310mm discs, 2-pot calipers, rear 285mm disc, 2-pot caliper
2009 Sprint ST 1050: Front 2 x 320mm discs, 4-pot calipers, rear 1 x 255mm disc, 2-pot caliper, ABS optional

Electrics
1993 Trident 900: 12v, 25A alternator
2000 Tiger 900: 12v, 40A alternator
2009 Sprint ST 1050: 12v alternator

Dimensions (L x W x H)
1993 Trident 900: 2152 x 760 x 1090mm
2000 Tiger 900: 2175 x 860 x 1345mm
2009 Sprint ST 1050: 2114 x 750 x 1215mm

Wheelbase
1993 Trident 900: 1510mm
2000 Tiger 900: 1550mm
2009 Sprint ST 1050: 1457mm

Seat height
1993 Trident 900: 775mm
2000 Tiger 900: 840/860mm
2009 Sprint ST 1050: 805mm

Weight (dry)
1993 Trident 900: 212kg
2000 Tiger 900: 215kg
2009 Sprint ST 1050: 210kg

Max speed
1993 Trident 900: 134mph
2000 Tiger 900: 128mph
2009 Sprint ST 1050: 161mph

Major model changes by year (years refer to model years, which start in October the previous year)
1991 All-new range of Hinckley Triumphs launched
1992 No major changes
1993 Trident Sprint, Tiger & Daytona 900 launched. Daytona 750/1000 dropped
1994 Speed Triple & Daytona Super III launched
1995 Thunderbird 900 launched
1996 Trophy 900/1200 revised with bigger twin-headlight fairing, Adventurer 900 launched. Speed Triple 750 (one year only)
1997 Daytona T595 & Speed Triple T509 launched. Sprint Sports & Executive launched
1998 Thunderbird Sport & Legend TT launched
1999 Sprint ST & Tiger injection launched, final batch of Daytona 1200SE's, Daytona 955i replaces T595, Speed Triple 955i replaces T509
2000 Sprint RS launched
2001 Tiger uprated to 955cc as 955i, Daytona uprated to 147bhp, Legend dropped.
2002 Sprint ST, Speed Triple and RS uprated to 118bhp. Adventurer dropped.
2003 Daytona has single-sided swing arm
2004 Special edition RS with belly pan, Panniers standard on Sprint ST, Thunderbird dropped.
2005 Speed Triple 1050 replaces 955i, Sprint ST 1050 replaces 955i
2006 No major changes
2007 Tiger 1050 replaces 955i, Speed Triple uprated to 131bhp, ST to 125bhp
2008 No major changes
2009 No major changes

The **Essential** Buyer's Guide™ series

£9.99*/$19.95*

*prices subject to change • p&p extra • for more details visit www.veloce.co.uk or email info@veloce.co.uk

Also from Veloce –

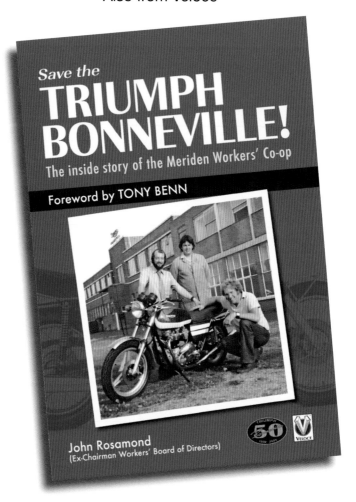

Save the
TRIUMPH BONNEVILLE!
The inside story of the Meriden Workers' Co-op

Foreword by TONY BENN

John Rosamond
(Ex-Chairman Workers' Board of Directors)

• Hardback • 22.5x15.2cm • £24.99 • 448 pages
• 116 colour & b/w pictures • ISBN: 978-1-845842-65-9

Written by the ex-Chairman of the Workers' Board of Directors of the famous Meriden Co-op, this is the real story of the last bastion of British motorcycle production following the collapse of the industry. It's also the story of a workforce's refusal to let the Triumph Bonneville die ...

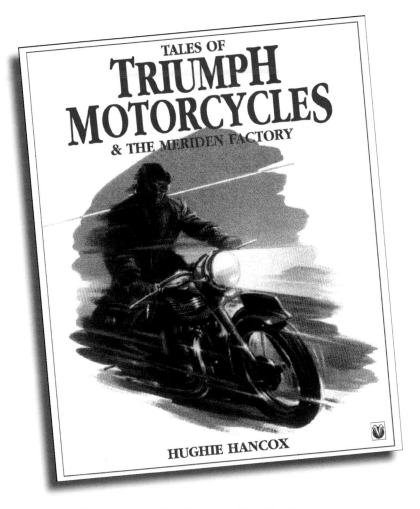

• Paperback • 25x20.7cm • £19.99 • 144 pages
• 91 b&w photos & illustrations • ISBN: 978-1-901295-67-2

Hughie worked at Triumph from 1954 until its closure in 1974. Here's the story of his life in the famous Meriden factory; of many adventures with Triumph motorcycles and Triumph people. Records the fascinating history of a great marque.

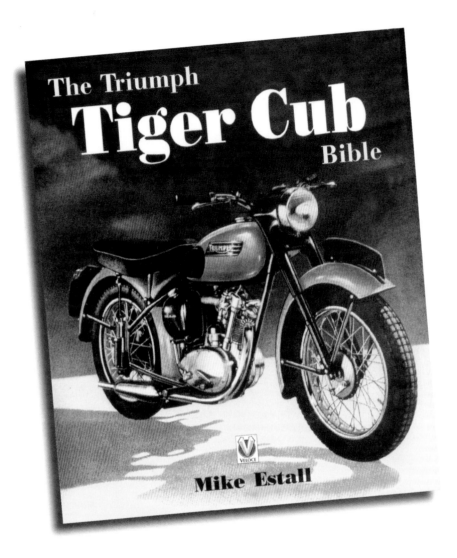

• Hardback • 25x20.7cm • £35.00 • 208 pages
• 210 b&w photographs • ISBN: 978-1-904788-09-6

The full history of the popular Triumph Cub motorcycle. This ultimate reference source book covers every aspect of these machines, including 22 detailed model profiles, delivery details, technical design specifications, military, police and competition bikes, plus the full story behind the model's production run.

*prices subject to change • p&p extra • for more details visit www.veloce.co.uk or email info@veloce.co.uk

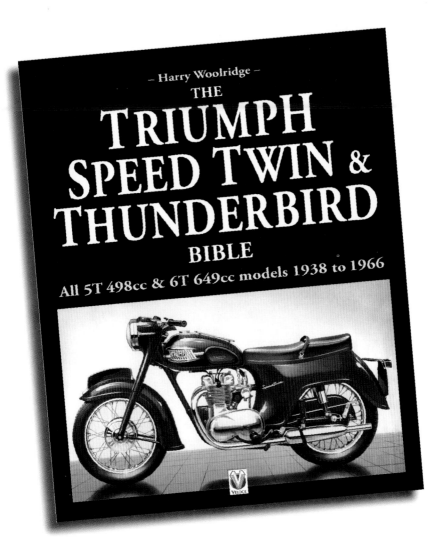

- Harry Woolridge -

THE
TRIUMPH
SPEED TWIN &
THUNDERBIRD
BIBLE

All 5T 498cc & 6T 649cc models 1938 to 1966

• Hardback • 25x20.7cm • £30.00 • 144 pages
• 142 photos • ISBN: 978-1-904788-26-3

The complete technical development history of the Triumph Speed Twin and
Thunderbird motorcycles, and an invaluable reference source to identification,
specification, exact year of manufacture and model type. A must for all Triumph
lovers.

*prices subject to change • p&p extra • for more details visit www.veloce.co.uk or email info@veloce.co.uk

Index